THE

FALSE

SELF

T0204285

Chapter One quotes

by

Bhagavan Sri Ramana Maharshi

Sri Nisargadatta Maharaj

Sri Annamalai Swami

Sri Muruganar

Sri Sadhu Om

Sri Vasistha

Sri Sankara

Chapters Two, Three, Four and Introduction

by

Anonymous Awareness

www.thefreedomreligionpress.com

www.seeseer.com

ISBN-13: 978-0-9797267-3-6

ISBN-10: 0-9797267-3-5

This book is sold with the understanding that the author's and publisher are not engaged in rendering psychological or medical advice. If expert assistance or counseling is required, the services of a licensed professional should be sought. The teachings and methods described in this book are of a religious or spiritual nature.

CONTENTS

INTRODUCTION   4

CHAPTER ONE   6
The Sages Quotes
about the false self

CHAPTER TWO   43
The Impostor

CHAPTER THREE   54
The Impostor's Tricks

CHAPTER FOUR   67
The Impostor's Tools

INTRODUCTION

Liberation or Self Realization can be defined as bringing the impostor self to its final end so that you can remain eternally as your true Self which is absolutely perfect Infinite-Awareness-Love-Bliss that has never experienced any sorrow or suffering in all of eternity.

The false self goes by many different names including:

A.   *Ego.*
B.   *Mind.*
C.   *Thought.*
D.   *Thinking.*
E.   *The impostor.*
F.   *Impostor self.*

The impostor self is very deceptive. In almost all humans the impostor self's desire to continue its imaginary existence is much greater than its desire to be brought to a final end. Therefore, the impostor self uses numerous preservation strategies to insure the continuation of its imaginary existence.

The impostor self has trillions of potential preservation strategies. There are as many potential preservation strategies as there are possible combinations of thoughts, beliefs, ideas, concepts and opinions.

The impostor self is thought and controls thinking. One of the impostor self's preservation strategies is to direct people's attention outward. Wasting time engaged in unnecessary activities when the time could have been better spent doing the most direct practice that leads to Liberation is a preservation strategy the impostor self uses.

Historically, the impostor self has almost always been successful. The impostor self has succeeded in enslaving almost all of the humans of the past. Not even one out of every one hundred million humans in the past has attained Liberation. This series of six books, The Self Realization Series, is for the purpose of conquering all of the obstacles to Liberation that the false self creates. The awakening of the extremely intense desire for Liberation will put an end to all of the impostor self's preservation strategies.

The Two Great Keys are:

1.   The awakening of the extremely intense desire for Liberation.

2.   Self honesty. Self honesty begins by actually seeing the impostor self's preservation strategies, tricks and deceptions.

The False self is Book Three in the Self Realization Series. One purpose of this series is to put just one category of quotes into a small book that has the advantage of making it easier to focus, meditate on, grasp and have insight into just one subject at a time. That makes the approach simple, easier and less complicated.

The idea is to stay focused on just one subject until you have received everything you need to receive from that one subject. Most people go on to the next subject without ever having learned to apply to their lives the subject they are studying now.

The Self Realization series of books are portable practice manuals aimed at helping sincere seekers of Self Realization master one Key to Self Realization at a time.

CHAPTER ONE

THE SAGES QUOTES

ABOUT

THE FALSE SELF

SRI RAMANA MAHARSHI
(525 – 545)

525.   So long as one retains a trace of individuality, one is a seeker still, and not a true seer effort free, even though one's penance and one's powers may be wonderful indeed.

526.   Poor fellow, you who are so proud of your omniscience, when you are questioned,
"You who know all things, do you know who you are?"
you collapse disgraced, discomfited.
O man of genius, may this your ego-mind dry up as dust
and perish utterly.

527.   Unless by one means or another mind dies out
and certitude from true Self-recognition comes,
the knowledge which mere learning brings
is like the horse's horn unreal.

528.   When ego ends, then one becomes a devotee true;
when ego ends, one becomes a knower too;
when ego ends one becomes Being supreme.
When ego ends, grace fills all space.

529.   Since every vice springs from the false pleasures of
swerving from the Self, the plentitude of virtue is the
perfect peace of pure awareness following the end of the ego
which is by such false pleasures fed.

530.   When ego goes, there is no loss of Being.
       Hence be not afraid.

531.   The separate ego wholly dead,
       the indivisible Self as pure awareness brightly shines.
       This I is not the false conceptual self
       earth-bound and body-bound.

532.   When the ego-life dissolves and dies in silence,
       then one lives the life supreme of pure awareness.
       When the false ego dream-like fades into its source,
       the true Self rises of its own accord.

533.   Great knowers recognize no other bondage
than the rising movements of the mind
and they find true release nowhere but in the total death,
leaving no trace behind,
of every movement of the mind.

534.   The false dream ends when we wake up.
       Even so, the ego dies when the sun, the true I, rises.
       Ego's destruction by strong Self-inquiry
       is what is known as Self-attainment.

535.   Only for those free from all sense of doership the bliss
of tranquil peace shines pure within. For the ego proud is the
sole evil seed whence spring all known calamities.

536.   Whether one is or one is not engaged in work,
one gains the state of non-action only when the ego with its
proud delusion "I am the doer" has died and disappeared.

537.   The bright Awareness, our true Being,
is the sole Truth the Heart should cherish.
The triads we perceive should be despised and driven away
as dreams created by the treacherous mind.

538.   Beside the Self nothing in truth exists.
        But then the deep delusion that the body is oneself
        makes one let go the solid, non-dual bliss of immortality
        and fall into birth and death.

539.   Of all the demonic qualities the basis is the ego.

540.   Those who have made the hardest sacrifice,
        that of the ego,
        have nothing more to renounce.

541.   Losing the false ego in awareness,
        and firm abidance as awareness
        is true clarity.

542.   Unlike the ego which rises and sets,
        the true Self abides for ever the same.
        Turn your back on the false ego, and so destroy it,
        and then shine as the one Self alone.

543.   Even as the ego does not die unless the Self's glance
falls on it, the painful dream of this phenomenal world will
never disappear unless the mind meets glorious death.

544.   The true light of Awareness
pure, subtle, egoless, non-objective, silent,
which tires the mind and baffles it till it admits "I know not",
this is Being-Awareness, this the Self.

545.   Here in this earthly life there is no greater good than
        gaining the grandeur of the Self supreme.
        To gain it and enjoy it, search within
        and first destroy the ego false and worthless.

SRI MURUGANAR
(546 – 559)

546.   The nature of my realization was such that the 'I' that
asserts its own reality was revealed as false and disappeared,
but not the 'I' that is the unique, pure, non-dual Self
that exists permeating all things equally.

547.   In the heart the absolute purity of imperishable grace
wells up as consciousness, the supreme,
so that the false deceitful mind that says 'I'
is destroyed and disappears,
no longer having any duality whatsoever to dwell upon.
I exist in the heart, with the heart itself as my real nature.

548.   In the hearts of true devotees
that are infused with the noble light of grace,
the dark ignorance of the ghostly ego, unable to operate,
will disappear.
In the mind in which the delusive and destructive ego
has completely died the
glory of grace will spontaneously shine forth in abundance.

549.   Other than being-consciousness there is no reliable support whatsoever for the soul. Grace itself is nothing less than this same being-consciousness. When the impetuous warring ego, which feeds on the mind's deceit, finally subsides in the heart, it is that same being-consciousness that manifests as the life of flooding grace.

550.   Until we eliminate the ghost-like ego –
the infatuation that arises through lack of Self-attention –
the unified consciousness of the Real will not arise. Similarly, until that unified consciousness of the Real arises,
the true love that is free of duality will not rise up in the heart.

551.   As long as we do not free ourselves from the state of inattention in which the unified state of the Self – that exists as pure consciousness – is subverted through the ego, the state of love that is the fullness of the Real, free of all differentiation, will not be experienced in the heart.

552.   The enlightened state, in which the grace and wisdom of the Self is directly experienced, will not come into being unless we separate ourselves from the illusory world of the divided mind so that it can no longer exist. Therefore we must thoroughly investigate and comprehend our own Self, so that the hostility of the ghost-like ego,
that brings with it the torment of an understanding
based on differentiation, may cease.

553.   Through tenacious inquiry into the Self the pure 'I' springs forth, eliminating the false personal identity.
We should realize that that true 'I', filled with the light of our own true nature, is the supreme reality itself.

554.   Dualistic concepts such as 'I' and 'He'
        are a treacherous trick of the mind
        that assumes the form of the body.
        Eliminate therefore this powerful mental imagination
        and discern the Self.

555.   Even now, if you entirely eradicate the personal ego
based on the multifarious nature of the non-Self,
you will experience an intense and limitless awakening,
as your true nature, the supreme Self, shines out.

556.   Realization in all its clarity flourished
        in the form of Self-consciousness,
        the light of Truth shining in the Heart
        as the vast expanse
        in which there is no arising of the contemptible ego.

557.   The death of the ego, which arises as 'I'
        in conjunction with the body's physical form,
        is synonymous with a new existence
        in the luminous firmament of the supreme,
        free of the embodied mind's forgetfulness of the Self.

558.   The ego self is like a poison which has its origin in
and thrives upon a fundamental misapprehension.
Here in the world it is an enemy masquerading as a friend
and you should root up and cast out every last vestige of it.

559.   Allow reality to shine as it truly is
        without any obstacle whatsoever
        by means of the destruction of the age-old deceit
        of the hostile ego.

560.   The substratum upon which the false idea of the mind has been superimposed is the Self.   When you see the mind, the Self, the underlying substratum, is not seen.   It is hidden by a false but persistent idea.   And, conversely, when the Self is seen there is no mind.

561.   Realizing the Self is the only useful and worthy activity in this life, so keep the body in good repair till that goal is achieved.   Afterwards, the Self will take care of everything and you won't have to worry about anything any more.   In fact, you won't be able to, because the mind that previously did the worrying, the choosing and the discriminating will no longer be there.   In that state you won't need it and you won't miss it.

562.   Questioner: So, you are saying that believing that I am a body and a particular person is purely imagination.
Or better still, a bad habit that I should try to go get rid of?

Annamalai Swami: Correct.   This habit has become very strong because you have reinforced and strengthened it over many lifetimes.   This will go if you meditate on your real Self. The habit will melt away, like ice becoming water.

563.   The mind only gets dissolved in the Self
        by constant practice.
        At that moment the 'I am the body' idea disappears,
        just as darkness disappears when the sun rises.

564. The body is not the Self;
the mind is not the Self.
The real 'I' is the Self,
and nothing ever happens to or affects the Self.

SRI SADHU OM
(565 – 567)

565. The happiness obtained
through the second kind of absorption,
the destruction of the mind,
is eternal.
It is the supreme bliss.

566. Temporary quiescence of the mind
is temporary quiescence of misery,
and permanent destruction of the mind
is permanent destruction of misery;
that is, the mind itself is misery!
Hence let us find out what is to be done to destroy the mind.

567. When Self, our nature of existence-consciousness,
instead of shining only as the pure consciousness 'I am',
shines mixed with an adjunct as 'I am a man, I am Rama,
I am so-and-so, I am this or that',
then this mixed consciousness is the ego.
This mixed consciousness can rise
only by catching hold of a name and form.
When we feel 'I am a man, I am Rama, I am sitting,
I am lying', is it not clear that we have mistaken the body
for 'I', and that we have assumed its name and postures as
'I am this and I am thus'?

568.   As to my mind, there is no such thing.

569.   When you believe yourself to be a person,
you see persons everywhere. In reality there are no persons,
only threads of memories and habits. At the moment of
realization the person ceases. Identity remains,
but identity is not a person, it is inherent in the reality itself.

570.   Of what use is the relative view to you?
You are able to look from the absolute point of view –
why go back to the relative? Are you afraid of the absolute?

571.   Questioner: I am engaged in the study of philosophy,
sociology and education. I think more mental development is
needed before I can dream of Self-realization.
Am I on the right track?

Maharaj: To earn a livelihood some specialized knowledge is
needed. General knowledge develops the mind, no doubt.
But if you are going to spend your life
in amassing knowledge, you build a wall round yourself.

To go beyond the mind, a well-furnished mind is not needed.

Questioner: Then what is needed?

Maharaj: Distrust your mind, and go beyond.

Questioner: What shall I find beyond the mind?

Maharaj: The direct experience of being, knowing and loving.

572.   I take my stand where no difference exists, where things are not, nor the minds that create them. There I am at home.

573.   As long as you do not see that it is mere habit, built on memory, prompted by desire, you will think yourself to be a person – living, feeling, thinking, active, passive, pleased or pained. Question yourself, ask yourself, 'Is it so?' 'Who am I?' 'What is behind and beyond all this?'
And soon you will see your mistake.

574.   There are so many who take the dawn for the noon,
        a momentary experience for full realization
        and destroy even the little they gain by excess of pride.

575.   The sun of truth remains hidden
        behind the cloud of self-identification with the body.

576.   The realized man is egoless; he has lost the capacity of identifying himself with anything. He is without location, placeless, beyond space and time, beyond the world.
Beyond words and thoughts is he.

577.   The false self must be abandoned
        before the real Self can be found.

578.   Resolutely remind yourself that you are not the mind
        and that its problems are not yours.

579.   That immovable state, which is not affected by the birth and death of a body or a mind, that state you must perceive.

580.   Have your being outside of this body of birth and death and all your problems will be solved. They exist because you believe yourself born to die. Undeceive yourself and be free. You are not a person.

581.   You have to be very alert, or else your mind will play false with you. It is like watching a thief – not that you expect anything from a thief, but you do not want to be robbed.

582.   Your personality dissolves
and only the witness remains.

583.   Any name or shape you give yourself
obscures your real nature.

584.   All your problems arise because you have defined and therefore limited yourself. When you do not think yourself to be this or that, all conflict ceases.

585.   There is no such thing as a person.

586.   Don't ask the mind to confirm what is beyond the mind. Direct experience is the only valid confirmation.

587.   Without Self-realization, no virtue is genuine.

588.   By looking tirelessly, I became quite empty
and with that emptiness all came back to me except the mind.

589.   Beyond the mind all distinctions cease.

590.   Questioner: How does one shape one's character?

Maharaj: By seeing it as it is, and being sincerely sorry.
This integral seeing-feeling can work miracles.

591.   The higher can be had
       only through freedom from the lower.

592.   Insanity is universal. Sanity is rare. Yet there is hope,
       because the moment we perceive our insanity,
       we are on the way to sanity.

593.   Questioner:
Yet we are afraid of the better and cling to the worse.

Maharaj: This is our stupidity, verging on insanity.

594.   The false self wants to continue – pleasantly.

595.   The only radical solution is to dissolve the separate
sense of 'I am such-and-such person' once and for good.

596.   The mind is a cheat.

597.   I know myself as I am in reality. I am neither the body,
nor the mind, nor the mental faculties. I am beyond all these.

598.   It is the 'I am the body' idea that is so calamitous.
       It blinds you completely to your real nature.
       Even for a moment do not think that you are the body.

599. Maharaj: When the mind is kept away from its preoccupations, it becomes quiet. If you do not disturb this quiet and stay in it, you find that it is permeated with a light and a love you have never known; and yet you recognize it at once as your own nature. Once you have passed through this experience, you will never be the same man again; the unruly mind may break its peace and obliterate its vision; but it is bound to return, provided the effort is sustained; until the day when all bonds are broken, delusions and attachments end and life becomes supremely concentrated in the present.

Questioner: What difference does it make?

Maharaj: The mind is no more. There is only love in action.

600. Trace every action to its selfish motive
and look at the motive intently till it dissolves.

601. Even the idea of being man or woman, or even human, should be discarded.

602. The person you became at birth and will cease to be at death is temporary and false. You are not the sensual, emotional and intellectual person,
gripped by desires and fears. Find out your real being.

603. It is the mind that tells you that the mind is there.
Don't be deceived. All the endless arguments about the mind are produced by the mind itself, for its own protection, continuation and expansion. It is the blank refusal to consider the convolutions and convulsions of the mind
that can take you beyond it.

604.   Keep on remembering: I am neither the mind nor its ideas. Do it patiently and with conviction and you will surely come to the direct vision of yourself as the source of being – knowing – loving, eternal, all-embracing, all-pervading.
You are the infinite focused in a body. Now you see the body only. Try earnestly and you will come to see the infinite only.

605.   You have never been, nor shall ever be a person.
       Refuse to consider yourself as one.

606.   The person is merely the result of a misunderstanding. In reality, there is no such thing. Feelings, thoughts and actions race before the watcher in endless succession, leaving traces in the brain and creating an illusion of continuity.
A reflection of the watcher in the mind creates the sense of 'I' and the person acquires an apparently independent existence. In reality there is no person, only the watcher identifying himself with the 'I' and the 'mine.'

607.   The sense of identity will remain, but no longer identification with a particular body. Being – awareness – love will shine in full splendor. Liberation is never of the person, it is always from the person.

608.   The person is but a shell imprisoning you.
       Break the shell.

609.   The reward of Self-knowledge
       is freedom from the personal self.

610.   The death of the mind is the birth of wisdom.

611.   I am not the mind, never was, nor shall be.

612.   When you know that you are neither body nor mind,
       you will not be swayed by them.

613.   The dissolution of personality is followed always by
a sense of great relief, as if a heavy burden has fallen off.

614.   It is not you who desires, fears and suffers,
it is the person built on the foundation of your body
by circumstances and influences. You are not that person.

615.   To know that you are a prisoner of your mind,
that you live in an imaginary world of your own creation,
is the dawn of wisdom. To want nothing of it,
to be ready to abandon it entirely, is earnestness.

616.   You must be free from the person
you take yourself to be, for it is the idea you have of yourself
that keeps you in bondage.

617.   Get busy with your ego – leave me alone.
       As long as you are locked up within your mind,
       my state is beyond your grasp.

618.   At present you are moved by
       the pleasure-pain principle which is the ego.

619.   The ego, like a crooked mirror,
narrows down and distorts. It is the worst of all the tyrants,
it dominates you absolutely.

620.   Freedom from the ego-self is the fruit of Self-inquiry.

621.   To be a person is to be asleep.

622.   What prevents you from knowing yourself as all and beyond all is the mind based on memory. It has power over you as long as you trust it; don't struggle with it; just disregard it. Deprived of attention, it will slow down and reveal the mechanism of its working. Once you know its nature and purpose, you will not allow it to create imaginary problems.

623.   Only when you know yourself as entirely alien to and different from the body, will you find respite from the mixture of fear and craving inseparable from 'I-am-the-body' idea.

624.   When the mind is quiet it reflects reality. When it is motionless through and through, it dissolves and only reality remains. This reality is so concrete, so actual, so much more tangible than mind and matter, that compared to it even diamond is soft like butter. This overwhelming actuality makes the world dreamlike, misty, irrelevant.

625.   With the dissolution of the personal 'I',
        personal suffering disappears.

626.   It is only your mind that prevents Self-knowledge.

627.   Rebel against your slavery to your mind,
        see your bonds as self-created
        and break the chains of attachment and revulsion.

628.   To be what you are, you must go beyond the mind, into your own being. It is immaterial what is the mind that you leave behind, provided you leave it behind for good. This again is not possible without Self-realization.

SRI VASISTHA
(629 – 768)

629.   Spreading the net of worldly objects of pleasure, it is this egotism that traps the living beings. Indeed, all the terrible calamities in this world are born of egotism. Egotism eclipses self-control, destroys virtue, and dissipates equanimity.

630.   It is this mind alone which is the cause of all objects of the world; the three worlds exist because of the mind-stuff; when the mind vanishes, the worlds vanish too.

631.   One's own mind has become one's worst enemy.
        Egotism is the foremost cause for evil.

632.   This diversity arises on account of mental modifications and it will cease when they cease.

633.   As long as one clings to the notion of the reality of "you" and "I", there is no liberation. Not by merely verbally denying such a notion of existence is it obliterated.

634.   Thought is mind;
        there is no distinction between the two.

635.   When the mind disintegrates, there is liberation,
and there is no more rebirth;
for it was mind alone that appeared to take birth and to die.

636.   Only a fool, not a wise man, is deluded by his own
ideas; it is a fool who thinks that the imperishable is
perishable and gets deluded. Egotism is but an idea, based on
a false association of the Self with the physical elements.

637.   Egotism promotes cravings; without it they perish.

638.   Abandon your reliance on fate or gods
       created by dull-witted people
       and by self-effort and Self-knowledge
       make the mind no-mind.

639.   When the mind is absorbed in the infinite consciousness
there is supreme peace; but when the mind is involved in
thoughts there is great sorrow. The restlessness of the mind
itself is known as ignorance or nescience; it is the seat of
tendencies, predispositions or conditioning –
destroy this through inquiry, as also by the firm abandonment
of contemplation of objects of sense-pleasure.

640.   "I", "mine" etc. have no existence at all;
       the one Self alone is the truth at all times.

641.   Do not get tangled with the moods of your mind,
but be established in truth. Regard the mind as a foreigner
or a piece of wood or stone. There is no mind in infinite
consciousness; that which is done by this non-existent mind
is also unreal. Be established in this realization.

642.   That the mind is impure
       is the experience of everyone who strives for liberation.

643.   Be established in truth and live in freedom
       in a mindless state.

644.   The notions of "I" and "mine"
are the eager receptacles which receive sorrow and suffering.
He who identifies the body with the Self sinks in misery.

645.   Worldliness sprouts from the seed of the ego-sense.

646.   Abandon this ego-sense
       with all the strength that lies within.

647.   The one infinite consciousness, which is of the nature of
       pure bliss, is eclipsed by the shadow of the ego-sense.

648.   All these notions of 'I' and 'you' are unreal.

649.   The practice of restraint
       bestows great joy and auspiciousness upon you.
       Hence, resort to self-restraint, give up ego-sense.

650.   Only the supreme truth exists
       and the individual personality is absorbed in it.

651.   This notion of the "I" cannot be got rid of
       except through Self-knowledge.

652.   Pursuing the inquiry into its real nature,
the mind abandons its identification even with the body.

653.   When the mind gets involved in
the external objective universe, it moves away from the Self.

654.   The mind is naught but ideas and notions.

655.   Reality is veiled by the mind
       and revealed when the mind ceases.

656.   In this world the cause of all misfortunes is only the mind which is full of sorrow and grief, desire and delusion. Forgetful of Self-knowledge, it generates desire and anger, evil thoughts and cravings which throw the person into the fire of sense-objects.

657.   When even the notion of the ego-sense has ceased,
       you will be like the infinite space.

658.   When the limited and conditioned feeling "I am so-and-so" ceases, there arises consciousness of the all-pervading infinite. Hence, you too abandon the false and fanciful notion of the ego-sense within your own heart. When this ego-sense is dispelled, the supreme light of Self-knowledge will surely shine in your heart.

This ego-sense alone is the densest form of darkness:
when it is dispelled, the inner light shines by itself.

659.   In truth, there is no mind.

660.   When the inner light begins to shine,
       the mind ceases to be,
       even as when there is light, darkness vanishes.

661. Be firmly established in egolessness
      and remain unpolluted like space.

662. The mind is the hub around which this vicious cycle
revolves, creating delusion in the minds of the deluded.
It is by firmly restraining that hub through intense self-effort
and keen intelligence, that the whole wheel is brought to a
standstill. When the hub's motion is stopped the wheel does
not revolve: when the mind is stilled, illusion ceases.
One who does not know this trick and does not practice it,
undergoes endless sorrow.

663. You will also enjoy freedom when the mind
ceases to be, along with the world-illusion contained in it.

664. Consciousness free from the limitations of the mind is
known as the inner intelligence: it is the essential nature of
no-mind, and therefore it is not tainted by the impurities of
concepts and percepts. That is the reality, that is supreme
auspiciousness, that is the state known as the supreme Self,
that is omniscience, and that vision is not had when the
wicked mind functions.

665. Be without the mind
      and realize that you are pure consciousness.

666. Mind is like a tree which is firmly rooted in the vicious
field known as body. Worries and anxieties are its blossoms;
it is laden with the fruits of old age and disease; it is adorned
with the flowers of desires and sense-enjoyments; hopes and
longings are its branches; and perversities are its leaves.

667.   Mind is like a crow which dwells in the nest of this
body. It revels in filth; it waxes strong by consuming flesh;
it pierces the hearts of others; it knows only its own point of
view which it considers as the truth; it is dark on account of its
ever-growing stupidity; it is full of evil tendencies;
and it indulges in violent expressions.
It is a burden on earth; drive it far, far away from yourself.

668.   Mind is like a monkey. It roams from one place
to another, seeking fruits (rewards, pleasures, etc.);
bound to this world-cycle it dances and entertains people.
Restrain it from all sides if you wish to attain perfection.

669.   Tranquillize the mind with the help of the mind itself.
For ever abandon every form of mental agitation.
Remain at peace within yourself
like a tree freed from the disturbance caused by monkeys.

670.   I am that which is indivisible, which has no name nor
change, which is beyond all concepts of unity and diversity,
which is beyond measure and other than which naught else is.
Hence, O mind, I abandon you who are the source of sorrow.

671.   Alas, for so long I have been victimized by ignorance:
but, luckily, I have discovered that which robbed me of
Self-knowledge! I shall never more be the victim of ignorance.

672.   In the absence of Self-knowledge, there arose ego-sense:
but now, I am free of ego-sense.

673.   After having abandoned the very root of the ego-sense,
I rest in the Self which is of the nature of peace.

674. The ego-sense is the source of endless sorrow, suffering
and evil action.

675. If the ego-sense ceases to be,
then the illusory world-appearance does not germinate again
and all cravings come to an end.

676. It is only a fool that entertains a feeling "This I am" in
relation to that temporary appearance known as the body etc.

677. It is my fault that I still cling to the notion that you,
my mind, is a real entity.
When I realize that all these phenomena
are illusory appearances, then you will become no-mind
and all the memories of sense-experiences, etc.
will come to an end.

678. It is by the destruction of the mind
that there can be happiness.

679. Mind is like a forest with thought-forms for its trees and
cravings for its creepers: by destroying these, I attain bliss.

680. Where there is Self-knowledge,
there is neither mind nor the senses,
nor the tendencies and habits (the concepts and percepts).
I have attained that supreme state.
I have emerged victorious. I have attained liberation.

681. Since all delusion has come to an end,
since the mind has ceased to be and all evil thoughts
have vanished, I rest peacefully in my own Self.

682.   When the mind has ceased to be because of the total absence of the notions of material existence, consciousness exists in its own nature as consciousness: and that is known as pure being.   When consciousness devoid of notions of objectivity merges in itself losing its separate identity as it were, it is pure being.   When all objects, external (material) and internal (notional) merge in consciousness, there is pure being of consciousness.   This is the supreme vision which happens to all liberated ones, whether they seem to have a body or they are without one.   This vision is available to one who has been "awakened", to one who is in a state of deep contemplation, and to a man of Self-knowledge;
it is not experienced by the ignorant person.

683.   There is no such thing as "I"
          nor "the world." There is no mind,
          nor an object of knowledge, nor the world-illusion.

684.   I am not the enjoyments, nor do they belong to me; this intellect and the sense-organs are not me, nor are they mine – they are inert and I am sentient.   I am not the mind which is the root-cause of this ignorant cycle of birth and death.

685.   The nature of enlightenment
          is known only by direct experience.

686.   So long as one does not subdue the mind with the mind,
          one cannot attain Self-knowledge; and as long as
          one entertains the false notions of "I" and "mine",
          so long sorrow does not come to an end.

687.   In the twinkling of an eye, this little ripple
        known as the mind assumes terrible proportions.

        Man foolishly ascribes to the Self
        the sorrow and the sufferings
        that do not touch it in the least
        and becomes miserable.

688.   All these that constitute the world-illusion come into
being like a mirage in the desert. This illusion spreads out like
waves in the ocean, assuming various names like mind,
the faculty of discrimination, the ego-sense,
the latent tendencies and the senses.
The mind and the ego-sense are not in fact two
but one and the same: the distinction is verbal. The mind is
the ego-sense and what is known as the ego-sense is the mind.

689.   Bring about the cessation of the mind.

690.   Mind and movement of thought are inseparable;
        and the cessation of one is the cessation of both.

691.   Mind should be destroyed.

692.   You do not exist, O mind.

693.   For a very long time, this ghost of a mind
generated countless evil notions like lust, anger, etc.
Now that that ghost has been laid,
I laugh at my own past foolishness.
The mind is dead; all my worries and anxieties are dead;
the demon known as ego-sense is dead.

694.   When the mind ceases to be, the craving ceases to be too. When the mind is dead and the craving is dead, delusion has vanished and egolessness is born.
Hence, I am awakened in this state of wakefulness.

695.   Thoughts are utterly useless, now that the mind is dead.

696.   O mind, when you cease to be, all the good and noble qualities blossom. There is peace and purity of heart. People do not fall into doubt and error. There is friendship which promotes the happiness of all. Worries and anxieties dry up. When the darkness of ignorance is dispelled, the inner light shines brightly. Mental distraction and distress cease, just as when the wind ceases to agitate its surface, the ocean becomes calm. There arises Self-knowledge within and the realization of truth puts an end to the perception of the world-illusion: the infinite consciousness alone shines.
There is an experience of bliss.

697.   The existence of the mind causes misery;
          and its cessation brings joy.

698.   As long there is mind, there is no cessation of sorrow.
When the mind ceases, the world-appearance also ceases
to be. The mind is the seed for misery.

699.   The very nature of the mind is stupidity.

700.   It is not possible to "kill the mind"
          without proper methods.

701.   Be free of the ego-sense and rejoice in the Self.

702.   As long as the concepts born of ignorance persist,
as long as there is perception of that which is not the infinite
and as long as there is hope in the trap known as the world,
so long one entertains notions of mind, etc.
As long as one considers the body as the "I" and as long as the
Self is related to what is seen, as long as there is hope
in objects with the feeling "this is mine",
so long there will be delusion concerning mind, etc.

703.   When incorrect perception has come to an end
and when the sun of Self-knowledge arises in the heart,
know that the mind is reduced to naught. It is not seen again.

704.   The mental conditioning has vanished.
        The mind has come to an end.

705.   The Self is not affected by the body,
        nor is the body in any way related to the Self.

706.   The individual is nothing more than the personalized
mind. Individuality ceases when that mind ceases.

707.   This ignorance has become dense by having been
expressed and experienced in thousands of incarnations,
within and outside this body by the senses. But, Self-
knowledge is not within the reach of the senses. It arises
when the senses and the mind, which is the sixth sense, cease.

708.   Give up this subservience
        to the ghost known as ego-sense and rest in the Self.

709.   You are the Self, not the mind.

710.   The goblin-mind residing in the body has nothing to do
       with the Self, yet it quietly assumes "I am the self."
       This is the cause of birth and death.
       This assumption robs you of courage.

711.   If it is realized that the perceived mind itself is unreal,
       then it is clear that the perceived world is unreal too.

712.   The mind of the knower of the truth is no-mind.

713.   He who is polluted by the ego-sense,
whether he is a learned scholar or one superior even to that,
he indeed is a wicked man.

714.   This creation is no doubt born of ignorance
and the belief in creation destroys true perception.
Though this creation is unreal, yet on account of the
emergence of the ego-sense, it appears to be solidly real.

715.   The cause of this world-appearance and bondage
       is indeed the mind.

716.   The best method is by inquiring into the nature of the
Self which is infinite. Your mind will be completely absorbed.
Then both the mind and the inquiry will cease.
Remain firmly established in what remains after that.

717.   This supreme consciousness alone exists.
       It is the supreme truth, untainted by any impurity,
       for ever in a state of perfect equilibrium
       and devoid of ego-sense. Once this truth is realized,
       it shines constantly without setting.

718.   I am pure consciousness,
       devoid of ego-sense and all-pervading.
       There is neither birth nor death for this consciousness.

719.   One thing still remains to be renounced:
       your ego-sense. If the heart abandons the mind,
       there is realization of the absolute.

720.   Worries (or movements of thought) alone
are known as mind.
Thought (notion, concept) is another name for the same thing.

721.   The utter destruction or extinction of the mind is the
extinction of the creation-cycle. It is also known as the
abandonment of the mind. Therefore, uproot this tree whose
seed is the "I"-idea, with all its branches, fruits and leaves,
and rest in the space in the heart.

722.   Realize "I am not that ego-sense"
       and rest in pure awareness.

723.   All notions cease. The falsity which arose as the mind
       ceases when notions cease.

724.   Ignorance lasts only so long as the mind functions.

725.   There is no mind in the liberated ones.

726.   Renunciation of the mind is total renunciation.

727.   The ego-sense is unreal. Do not trust it.

728.   The ego-sense looks upon space around it as itself and its possession.   Thus it identifies itself with the body, etc. which it desires to protect.   The body, etc. exist and perish after some time.   On account of this delusion, the ego-sense grieves repeatedly, thinking that the self is dead and lost. When the pot, etc. are lost, the space remains unaffected. Even so, when the bodies are lost, the Self remains unaffected. The Self is pure consciousness, subtler than even space. It is never destroyed. It is unborn. It does not perish.

729.   Remain in the pure, egoless state.

730.   The notion "I am the body" is bondage; the seeker should avoid it.   "I am no-thing but pure consciousness" – such understanding when it is sustained is conducive to liberation. It is only when one does not realize the Self which is free from old age, death, etc. that one wails aloud, "Alas, I am dead or I am helpless."   It is by such thoughts that ignorance is fortified.   Free your mind from such impure thoughts and notions. Rest in the Self free from such notions.

731.   When the ego-sense dies, ignorance perishes
         and that is known as liberation.

732.   All these notions exist in the mind.
Subdue the mind by the mind. Purify the mind by the mind. Destroy the mind by the mind.

733.   When the movement of the mind has ceased,
         the Self shines by its own light.
         In that light all sorrow comes to an end
         and there is the bliss which the Self experiences in itself.

734.   I am THAT which is beyond the body, mind and senses.

735.   The abandonment of notions is the supreme good.

736.   The non-perception of objects
and the non-arising of notions. This should be experienced.

737.   When the mind abandons its conditioning,
        the objects lose their temptation.

738.   One who has not abandoned the ego-sense and
mine-ness knows neither renunciation nor wisdom nor peace.

739.   The supreme Self is in the supreme Self,
the infinite in the infinite, the peace in peace.
That is all there is, neither "I" nor "the world" nor "the mind."

740.   When the seed for the world-appearance (which is the
ego-sense) has been destroyed, the world-appearance goes
with it. Even as the mirror gets misted by moisture, the Self is
veiled by the unreal ego-sense. This ego-sense gives rise to all
the rest of this world-appearance. When it goes, then the Self
shines by its own light, even as the sun shines when the
veiling cloud is blown away.

741.   Just as an object thrown into the ocean dissolves in the
ocean, the ego-sense which enters the Self is dissolved in it.

742.   Self-knowledge is the realization of the unreality of the
        ego-sense. Nothing else can ensure your true welfare.
        Hence, first abandon the individualized ego-sense.

743. Know that all that you experience in the name of mind,
ego-sense, intellect, etc. is nothing but ignorance.
This ignorance vanishes through self-effort.

744. Wherever the ego-sense arises there the world manifests
itself. The ego-sense is the first cause of this world-illusion.

745. If one is able to remove the ego-sense by means of one's
awakened intelligence, he cleanses from his consciousness
the impurity known as world-appearance.

746. The men of wisdom perceive that
the entire creation is hidden in the ego-sense.

747. If the I-ness or ego-sense ceases in you,
you will remain like the space and there will be peace.

748. The ego-sense that perceives the diversity
is the creator of the division. The ego-sense is bondage
and its cessation is liberation. It is so simple.

749. "I am the body" is delusion, not truth.
You are the pure Self or undivided consciousness.

750. The notion of "I" is utter ignorance;
it blocks the path to liberation.

751. When a dream-object perishes, nothing is lost:
when "the world" or "the I" is lost, nothing is lost.

752. The abandonment of ego-sense is
the cessation of ignorance; this and nothing else is liberation.

753.   The ego-sense is unreal though it appears to be real.

754.   On examination, even the body, etc. are seen to be
unreal and false. When even the mind has ceased with
the cessation of notions concerning the body and the world,
the Self or the infinite consciousness alone remains.

755.   Matter and mind are identical; and both are false. You
are deluded by this false appearance. Self-knowledge will
dispel this delusion. Both Self-knowledge and the cessation
of world-appearance are the characteristics of wisdom.

756.   In the infinite and unmodified or unconditioned
consciousness modification is impossible;
the conditioning is but a false notion. Therefore,
it melts away in the heart of one who has Self-knowledge
and who is free from delusion and ego-sense.

757.   To the wise there is neither ego-sense nor the world.

758.   The Self alone is real, devoid of the concepts of time,
space and such other notions; the Self is not a void.
This truth is realized only by those who are established
in the supreme state, not by those who rest in the ego-sense.

759.   Human beings are narrow-minded and petty minded,
       interested in the trivia of life.
       They spend most of their time in pursuit of evil desires.

760.   They are tempted away from the path
       of order and wisdom by their own vanities and desires.

761. Among human beings there are liberated ones.
      But they are extremely rare.

762. Though the body is experienced to be real,
      it does not exist in truth.

763. You are not this little personality.

764. Limitless is this ignorance with countless branches in all
directions; it cannot come to an end by any means other than
Self-knowledge.

765. "I am not a wave, I am the ocean" –
      when thus the truth is realized, the wave-ness ceases.

766. The mind itself appears to be the objects of perception,
      just as in dream.

767. The physical or material universe
      does not exist at any time anywhere.
      The subtle body itself appears to be the solid body
      on account of the notion of such solidity
      arising in it repeatedly.
      Its very source is unreal.

768. For one who rests in his own Self
      and rejoices in the Self,
      in whom cravings have ceased and ego-sense is absent,
      life becomes non-volitional and there is perfect purity.

      One in millions, however,
      is able to reach this unconditioned state of pure being.

769.   This body is the product of food, and constitutes
the material sheath. It depends on food and dies without it.
It is a mass of skin, flesh, blood, bones and uncleanness.
It is not fit to see as oneself, who is ever pure.

770.   One's true Self shines forth again
          when the contamination is removed.

771.   Eliminate completely your self-identification with this
body, and with determination see that your mind is devoted
to the removal of all ideas of additions to your true Self.

772.   So long as even a dreamlike awareness of yourself as an
individual in the world remains, as a wise person persistently
see to the removal of all ideas of additions to your true Self.

773.   The tendency to see "me" and "mine" in the body and
the senses, which are not oneself, must be done away with
by the wise by remaining identified with one's true Self.

774.   The wise who have experienced reality
          call the mind ignorance.

775.   The sage who stands in the Eternal, the Self of being,
          ever full, of the secondless bliss of the Self,
          has none of the hopes fitted to time and space
          that make for the formation of a body of skin, and flesh,
          subject to dissolution.

776. Drawing near to the eternal, stainless awakening,
whose nature is bliss, put very far away this disguise
whose nature is inert and foul.

777. Outward attachment arises through sensual objects;
inward attachment, through personality.
Only he who, resting in the Eternal, is free from passion,
is able to give them up.

778. There is no other danger for him who knows,
but this wavering as to the Self's real nature.
Thence arises delusion, and thence selfish personality;
thence comes bondage, and therefrom sorrow.

779. Bringing to an end the activity of the selfish personality,
all passion being laid aside when the supreme object is
gained, rest silent, enjoying the bliss of the Self,
in the Eternal, through the perfect Self, from all doubt free.

780. When the false self ceases utterly,
and the motions of the mind caused by it come to an end,
then, by discerning the hidden Self,
the real truth that "I AM THAT" is found.

781. When free from the grasp of selfish personality,
he reaches his real nature;
Bliss and Being shine forth by their own light.

782. Man's circle of birth and death
comes through the fault of attributing reality to the unreal,
but this false attribution is built up by mind;
this is the effective cause of birth and death and sorrow.

783. Man's circle of birth and death is built by mind,
and has no permanent reality.

784. There is no unwisdom,
except in the mind,
for the mind is unwisdom,
the cause of the bondage to life;
when this is destroyed,
all is destroyed;
when this dominates,
the world dominates.

785. Thinking things not Self are "I" –
this is bondage for a man;
this,
arising from unwisdom,
is the cause of falling into
the weariness of birth and dying.

CHAPTER TWO

THE IMPOSTOR

1. These are the definitions of the words ego,
    Self and thought that will be used in this book:

2. THOUGHT:
    Thoughts are the words of your language in your mind.

3. If your native language is English
    and you write in English and speak English,
    those same English words in your mind are thoughts.

4. If you are fluent in two languages, then the words of
    those two languages in your mind is thought.

5. EGO: ego is the thought I.

6. The ego is the "I thought."

7. "I am happy." "I am sad." "I did this." "I did that."
    There are so many sentences in thought that contain the word
    "I." That thought "I" in each of those sentences is the ego.

8. The ego is the idea of a separate, individual identity.

9. The ego identifies with the body and with thought
    and calls the body and thought "I."

10. The ego is thought.

11.   The ego is thinking.

12.   SELF: the Self is infinite-eternal-awareness-love-bliss.
Those are five words pointing towards one awareness.
Awareness-love-bliss are not three, they are one.

13.   The Self is the background of awareness.

14.   Because almost all humans
are in the habit of looking outward towards thoughts,
the body, the world, people, places, things, etc.,
it *appears* as though the background of awareness (the Self)
wakes up in the morning and goes to sleep at night.

15.   If you turn your attention towards
the background of awareness, eventually you will discover:
the background of awareness is continuous.

16.   Because almost all humans
are in the habit of looking outward towards thoughts,
the body, the world, people, places, things, etc.,
it *appears* as though the background of awareness is limited.

17.   If you turn your attention towards the awareness that
wakes up in the morning, instead of towards people, places,
things, thoughts, etc., eventually you will discover
that awareness is infinite-eternal-awareness-love-bliss.

18.   The background of awareness
        that wakes up in the morning
        is there during all the waking hours
        until one goes to sleep at night.

19. Thoughts come and go, but the background of
awareness that is aware of the thoughts is there
during all the waking hours and does not come and go.

20. The background of awareness is the true Self.

21. Before you learned the language you now think in,
the background of awareness was there.

22. Then you learned the word "I" in your language.

23. Your body was given a name and when people saw that body they said "There goes John" (or Mike, or Jane, or Julie, or Kumar, or Radha) or whatever name they gave your body.

24. Thus the idea arose "I am John, I am this body."

25. You existed as the background of awareness
before that I-thought arose.

26. The thought calling its "self" "I" is an impostor "self."

27. The background of awareness is the true Self.

28. The fact that you existed before you learned the
language that became your thoughts helps to reveal
the difference between your true Self and the impostor.

29. Because you existed as the background of awareness
before you learned the language
that produced the thoughts you now think in,
you can easily see that the thought "I" is an impostor.

30. All thoughts are opposed to your real nature.

31. You know that thoughts are not part of your true nature
because you had to learn them.

32. That is why you cannot speak, write and think fluently
in two hundred different languages:
because you have not acquired those languages.

33. You can observe that same process in an infant.

34. You can see that an infant is aware
before it learns any language.

35. You can observe the child growing older
and learning a language.

36. You can observe when the child learns the word "I"
and when the child begins to say the word "I."

37. Being able to see how the impostor arose in you
and how the impostor arises in every human infant and child
is a very important tool.

38. The reason it is a very important tool is:
you do not have to rely upon someone else
to tell you that the ego is an acquired impostor.

39. You can observe this for yourself.

40. Thought is something foreign, alien to the true Self.

41. Thought pretends to be the Self.

42. Thought is not the Self.

43. Thought is an impostor.

44. Thought believes thought is a real entity
and thought believes thought is a real self.

45. Thought is not a real entity and thought is not a self.

46. Living from thought instead of living from Awareness
is the cause of all human suffering.

47. The impostor (thought – ego)
is the cause of all human problems, sorrow and suffering.

48. The background of awareness is the true Self.

49. The awareness, that *appears* to wake up in the morning,
is the true Self.

50. The awareness that is looking through your eyes now
is the true Self.

51. As an example for clarification, you could view
thinking and memory as something like a computer program.

52. Within that computer program is a virus.

53. The virus is called the "I thought."

54. The virus controls the program.
The "I thought" controls all thinking.

55. The virus pretends to be your self.
The "I thought" pretends to be your self.

56. The virus creates tremendous sorrow and suffering.
The "I thought" creates tremendous sorrow and suffering.

57. None of the sorrow or suffering is needed.

58. What is needed is to delete the virus that pretends to be your self. What is needed is to delete the impostor self.

59. When one attempts to delete the virus,
the virus creates many thoughts
claiming that deleting the virus is not a good idea.

60. The virus has many strategies
to preserve the illusion that it is real
and to continue the delusion that it is the real self.

61. In humans the program that came from the outside
and took control of their awareness
is called thought, language, and thinking.

62. In humans the virus is called the ego or the "I thought."

63. The "I thought" (ego)
is an impostor pretending to be the Self.

64. The ego is the cause of all human sorrow and suffering.

65.   The ego is the cause of all disease, death, war, fear,
        anger and violence.

66.   Although many thousands of years have passed,
        human beings have made almost no inward progress
        toward ending suffering, sorrow, war, fear, anger,
        violence, cheating and lying.

67.   Thousands of years ago humans had suffering, sorrow,
        war, fear, anger, violence, cheating and lying.

68.   Now, today, currently, humans have suffering, sorrow,
        war, fear, anger, violence, cheating and lying.

69.   What has kept humans
        in the same pool of inward unsolved problems?

70.   The ego (the impostor) has kept humans
        in the same pool of inward unsolved problems.

71.   Inward problems cannot be solved by looking outward.

72.   Inward problems can only be solved by looking inward.

73.   The ego knows that if the attention is turned inward,
        the ego will be found to be a myth, an impostor,
        an illusion, a delusion, a dream.

74.   Therefore, due to the ego's fear of ending,
        the ego keeps the attention directed outward.

75.   Usually when people attempt to turn the attention inward, they are still looking outward because they do not understand the meaning of looking inward. Observing thoughts, feelings or desires is not looking inward. Only awareness observing awareness is looking inward.

76.   All humans are slaves
        and the impostor "self" is their master.

77.   Exposing the preservation strategies of that impostor "self", how to put an end to those strategies, how to bring the impostor "self" to an end, thus ending all suffering and sorrow and remaining in the true Self whose nature is infinite-eternal-awareness-love-bliss, are the primary purposes of this Self Realization series of books.

78.   Ending the ego does not end the body.

79.   After the ego ends,
        the body will live out the natural course of its life.

80.   One should never attempt to harm the body.

81.   The ego is the "I thought."

82.   Ending the ego is ending the "I thought."

83.   Ending the bodily life will not end the ego.

84.   The ego will create the dream of a new body
        when the old body ends.

85.   Thus,
      ending the body does not help to solve the problems.

86.   Humans almost always have their attention
      directed outward towards thoughts, people,
      places, things, experiences, etc.

87.   The background of awareness is the true Self
      and humans almost always ignore it.

88.   Your true Self deserves your attention.

89.   When humans turn their attention away from thoughts,
the body, the world, people, places, things, experiences, etc.
and towards their awareness,
eventually they will directly experience their true Self.

90.   The impostor (thought) pretending to be your self
      and calling its pretend self "I"
      should not be tolerated even for one moment.

91.   Especially an impostor
that has created so much suffering and sorrow
should not be tolerated even for one moment. For example,
all of the trillions of acts of violence throughout
human history were created by the impostor self. All human
sorrow and suffering is created by the impostor self.

92.   The impostor (thought) is like a parasite.

93.   Because the ego believes it is a real entity,
      the ego is afraid of ending.

94.   The ego controls all thinking.

95.   Because the ego is afraid of ending
       and controls all thinking, the ego directs thought
       in ways that will preserve its imaginary self
       so that its imaginary self is not brought to an end.

96.   The purpose of the teachings in this Self Realization
series of books is to bring the impostor to an end
so that what remains is only the true Self whose nature is
Absolutely Perfect Infinite-Eternal-Awareness-Love-Bliss.

97.   When the impostor ends,
       all suffering and sorrow also end.

98.   Imagining that thinking or thought is your self
       is a delusion, a dreamlike illusion.

99.   Thinking that you are a body living in a world
       is a delusion, a dreamlike illusion.

100.   Thought has created those delusions.

101.   All sorrow, suffering and delusions
       have one single root.

102.   The single root is thought.

103.   The root of thought is the "I thought."

104.   The root of thought is the thought "I."

105.   Thought is not part of your true nature.
        Thought is something you learned.

106.   Do not allow something you acquired
        to pretend to be your self.

107.   Try this experiment:
        Set aside two hours
        when you have no other activities going on.
        Sit down in a place where you will not be disturbed.
        Shut your eyes.
        Make a decision that for the next two hours
        you will not allow a single thought to arise.
        If you are really in control of thinking,
        then not even one thought will arise.
        If thinking controls you,
        then even though you have made the decision
        not to allow a single thought to arise,
        you will not be able to sit for two hours
        without a single thought arising.
        What a revelation this can be
        to discover that thought,
        something that you acquired,
        now controls you!

108.   The book you are reading now,
        The False self,
        contains a description of the secret
        that has enslaved humanity
        for as long as there have been humans.

CHAPTER THREE

THE IMPOSTOR'S TRICKS

1.   The ego controls all thinking.

2.   The ego can create an argument against anything.

3.   Therefore,
reserve all arguments against what is being presented here
until you have read the book at least three times.

4.   Otherwise, the ego will generate arguments
        against any anti-ego presentation,
        thus blocking what is being presented.

5.   See the vicious circle:

6.   The ego in its attempts to prevent the ego
        from being exposed for the impostor that it is,
        and to block the realization that
        the ego is the cause of all human sorrow and suffering,
        creates arguments against what is revealed in this book.

7.   Because the ego sets the standards for the debate,
        the ego always wins the debate.

8.   The way to break that vicious circle
        is to delay all arguments against what is presented here
        until you have read the book very slowly
        at least three times.

9.   When the ego forms an argument
      against something in this book,
      see the argument as an ego preservation strategy
      and ignore it,
      postponing all argument
      until the presentation is complete.

10.   Having the motivation to understand,
      instead of the motivation to argue,
      will help to produce an insight
      into what is being presented here.

11.   Put the arguments on hold
      until you have read the book at least three times.

12.   By that time you may be so skilled at recognizing
      the ego's preservation strategies,
      you may decide to delay the arguments forever.

13.   At least give what is being presented here a fair chance
      by being aware of the arguments that the ego creates
      and disregarding those arguments
      until an insight into what is revealed here is awakened.

14.   Plenty of time to argue later,
      after reading the entire book.

15.   The ego has been deceiving humans
      for as long as there have been humans.

16.   Be aware of the ego's attempts to deceive you.

17.   The ego controls all thinking, therefore,
various combinations of thoughts, ideas, beliefs and opinions are the ego's primary tools to preserve the ego's imaginary "self" and to prevent you from discovering your true Self.

18.   Most humans have never observed
        the background of awareness, not even for one second.

19.   Therefore, whatever opinions most people have about what the background of awareness is, what its qualities are, what the true Self is, etc., have no basis.

20.   If you observe the background of awareness
        for many hours every day, for a number of years,
        then you will eventually know that your awareness is
        infinite-eternal-awareness-love-bliss.

21.   Because most humans spend their entire lives looking outward at thoughts, the body, the world, people, places, things, etc., most humans never observe their own awareness, not even for one moment, in their entire lifetimes.

22.   Concepts, beliefs and conclusions
        are not truly important.
        What is truly important is Direct Experience.

23.   Be aware of your thoughts, ideas, beliefs and opinions
        and see how they serve the ego.

24.   See Chapter Two for a clarification of
        the difference between the ego and the true Self.

25.   Read the books in this Self Realization series
       as a guide to Direct Experience.
       Never read an authentic Direct Path Teaching
       as a theory for intellectual entertainment.

26.   Because the ego is afraid of ending,
the ego directs and creates thoughts,
ideas, concepts, beliefs and opinions
that will help the ego to continue its illusion of being real
and that will prevent the ego from being brought to an end.

27.   Those thoughts, ideas, concepts, beliefs and opinions
are ego preservation strategies.
Ego preservation strategies can also be called the ego's tricks.

28.   Because thoughts can be combined
       in trillions of combinations,
       the ego can create trillions of preservation strategies.

29.   The ego has the ability
       to hide what it is doing from itself.

30.   The ego creates ego preservation strategies
throughout the entire day.
Most people are not aware of the ego's preservation strategies.

31.   If you are not aware of
       how the ego preserves its imaginary self,
       then the ego succeeds in preserving its imaginary self.

32.   In your day to day life watch carefully to see how the ego preserves its imaginary self. For example, watch how the ego leads you into unnecessary activities instead of spiritual practice. Look at the rationalizations, excuses and reasons that the ego creates to justify your engaging in unnecessary activities. Stopping all unnecessary activities creates more time for spiritual practice.

33.   If one million people study a spiritual teaching and only one of those people ends the ego illusion, why did the other nine hundred ninety-nine thousand, nine hundred ninety-nine miss the opportunity?

34.   The reason the other nine hundred ninety-nine thousand nine hundred ninety-nine people missed the opportunity is because of the ego's fear of ending.

35.   Due to the ego's fear of ending,
        the ego creates strategies to preserve its imaginary self.

36.   Distorting spiritual teachings is one of the many
        strategies the ego uses to preserve its imaginary self.

37.   People project their own thoughts, ideas, concepts, opinions, beliefs and interpretations unto the spiritual teachings they are studying. When those interpretations etc. are added to the Teaching, the Teaching is no longer the Teaching. When studying the Direct Path Teachings be aware of when you are adding your own thoughts and interpretations. Say to yourself "Those are my thoughts. Now without my ideas, opinions, beliefs, conclusions and interpretations, what does the Teaching actually state?"

38. Right from the beginning,
the ego's preservation strategies have to be dealt with.

39. If the ego's preservation strategies are not dealt with,
the ego will block out or distort what is revealed
in the spiritual teaching you are studying.
Most attempts at awakening fail because of failure
to put an end to the ego's preservation strategies.

40. The ego's preservation strategies
can be brought to an end.
One of the purposes of this Self Realization series of books is
to teach how to put an end to the ego's preservation strategies.

41. Usually any mention of exposing the ego's preservation
strategies makes the ego run the other way.
In most people the ego hides its preservation strategies
from its imaginary self.

42. Being willing to look at the ego's preservation strategies
is a sign of spiritual maturity.

43. Most people are not willing to look at
the ego's preservation strategies.

44. Reading a book that reveals some of the ego's
preservation strategies will not make you immune to them.
You have to actually put the Self Realization Teachings into
practice to bring the ego's preservation strategies to an end.

45. One of the ego's preservation strategies is the thought
"This does not apply to me."

46.   The ego is very tricky and deceptive in all humans. The ego is a liar in all humans. The ego lies to its imaginary self.

47.   When something is pointed out in this book and you think "This does not apply to me," take a second look.

48.   Maybe it does apply to you
and the ego is blocking that fact out as a preservation strategy.

49.   Challenge the thought "This does not apply to me."

50.   The thought "This does not apply to me"
        may be an ego preservation strategy.

51.   One of the differences between
the one out of a million who awakens and the others
who do not is the ability to stay focused on an essential point
until it becomes an insight and a tool that you can use.

52.   An intellectual understanding of what is revealed
in this Self Realization series of books is only the first step.
The second step is to go beyond thought to awaken insight.

53.   The Self Realization series of books are
filled with the insights that lay the foundation for you to be
the one who awakens and not one of the millions who miss.

54.   Dwell on what is written
        in every sentence in every chapter of every book
        in the Self Realization Series
        until insights are awakened
        that become tools you can use.

55.   To awaken insight, don't read what is written in the Self Realization series the way you read a newspaper or trivia, and don't read for the purpose of gathering information.

56.   To awaken insight,
read as though you were reading instructions about how to fly that are vital to prevent you from crashing.

57.   Slowly reflect on each sentence.

58.   That is why the sentences are numbered with a space between them: to encourage you to reflect slowly on each sentence, to pause, and not to hurry to the next sentence.

59.   Continue to reread long after
       the intellect has understood the meaning of the words.

60.   Reading very, very slowly is insight reading.

61.   Read very slowly. Then read at an even slower pace,
       allowing you to look deeply into each sentence,
       and to see what each sentence points towards.

62.   The ego is like an inchworm that lets go of one thought
       only when it has grabbed hold of the next thought.

63.   Therefore,
when rereading every sentence many times over and over,
don't be in a hurry to proceed to the next sentence.
Stay with each sentence for a long time
before reading the next sentence.

64.   It is important to understand the difference between insight and intellectual understanding.

65.   Never confuse intellectual understanding with insight.

66.   Intellectual understanding,
which means understanding the words, is good as a first step.

67.   However, after one has understood the words, if one then goes on to another concept before the insight has awakened, the words may become obstacles and hindrances, instead of tools that end the ego.

68.   Intellectual "understanding", an intellectual appetite and an intellectual approach to "spirituality"
are what characterize the nine hundred ninety-nine thousand nine hundred ninety-nine who miss.

69.   Insight is the approach used by the one in a million who brings the ego to its final end.

70.   Most people study "spiritual" teachings because they enjoy the concepts.

71.   The ego is fundamentally dishonest in humans and the ego has the ability to hide what it is doing from its imaginary "self."

72.   Therefore, many people fail to see that their primary reason for studying "spiritual" teachings is because they enjoy the concepts.

73. The desire to go quickly to the next concept and to gather more and more information and to read thousands of spiritual books and to think about what has been read and to discuss what has been read and thought about, are symptoms of the intellectual appetite and intellectual "spirituality".

74. Approaching the study of spiritual teachings intellectually, as just described (73), is an approach used by the nine hundred ninety-nine thousand nine hundred ninety-nine who miss.

75. One of the ego's tricks is to get lost in spiritual concepts, opinions, philosophies or beliefs.

76. The report of Direct Experience by those who have brought the impostor self to its final end and practical, clearly and directly communicated instructions teaching how to bring the impostor self to its final end is what is of true value to those extremely rare and extremely few sincere seekers of Self Realization.

77. Ideas are not what this Self Realization series of books point towards.

78. These books point towards the awareness that is prior to thought, and how to directly experience that awareness.

79. The ego likes to scatter attention.

80. Scattering attention is one of the ego's preservation strategies.

81.   Thinking scatters attention.

82.   To bring the attention to a single point
and to dwell on that single point for a very long time
is the way to awaken insight.

83.   Insight is not thinking and insight is not belief.

84.   Insight is a permanent new perspective.

85.   To find one powerful quote (not a quote that the
spiritually immature ego selects in its efforts to preserve itself)
and to stay with that quote until insight awakens,
is the kind of approach used by the one in a million
who brings the ego to its final end.

86.   One might stay with a single quote for one day
or one week or much longer than one week.
Those who use this approach are rare.

87.   Keeping the attention directed outward
is one of the ego's fundamental tricks.

88.   Creating unnecessary activities is one way
the ego keeps the attention directed outward
and is another of the ego's tricks.

89.   Dropping all unnecessary activities
to create the maximum amount of time for spiritual practice is
an essential key to success in bringing the ego to its final end.

90. Pretending that a journey through thought
is an authentic spiritual journey is also one of the ego's tricks.

91. The ego has as many tricks to draw upon
as there are concepts, ideas, beliefs and opinions.

92. Choosing belief instead of Direct Experience
is one of the ego's tricks.

93. Wasting time is one of the ego's tricks.

94. Spending time in entertainment that could have been
spent in spiritual practice is one of the ego's tricks.

95. Almost all thoughts are just the ego's tricks.

96. Reflect on one sentence for a very long time
before reading the next sentence.

97. Reflecting means looking.

98. Reflecting does not mean thinking
and reflecting does not mean arguing.

99. Stay with each sentence until you have an insight into it.

100. The previous sentence (99) describes a key approach
used by the one in a million who succeeds in living in
infinite-eternal-awareness-love-bliss.

101. There are a few key principles to be understood
and some reading may be required for that.

102. Be very careful when choosing
     which spiritual books to read.

     Almost all of the spiritual teachings from the past
     were created by the ego
     for the purpose of preserving the ego's imaginary self.

Those spiritual teachings that were not created by the ego
were immediately distorted by the ego to serve the ego.

     The result is the same either way:

     Almost all of the spiritual teachings from the past
     serve the ego.

103. Discussing and thinking about spiritual teachings
     are ego preservation strategies
     (tricks created by the ego to preserve its imaginary self).

104. The ego continues thinking about spiritual concepts
     to avoid the practice that leads to the ego's final end.

105. The ego keeps people lost
     in an endless maze of concepts.

106. Spiritual concepts do not lead to freedom.

107. Only practice leads to freedom.

108. However,
     it must be the most rapid and direct spiritual practice
     and not a practice created by or distorted by the ego.

CHAPTER FOUR

THE IMPOSTOR'S TOOLS:

THOUGHT, THINKING AND BELIEFS

1.   Thought is the primary tool the ego uses
to preserve its imaginary self.

2.   Therefore, it is important to see how the ego
uses thought to create ego preservation strategies.

3.   First one must understand the nature of thinking,
thought, concepts and beliefs and the myths the ego
has created about thinking, thought, concepts and beliefs.

4.   Thought is not a means to discover the absolute Truth.

5.   The ego has convinced
almost all humans and almost all spiritual aspirants
that thought is a means to know the absolute Truth.

6.   Some people think they already know
that thought is not a means to know the absolute Truth.

7.   Almost all of those people are still trying to use thought
as a means to know the absolute Truth.

8.   This reveals that they do not really know
that thought is not a means to know the absolute Truth.

9.   They have confused knowing-insight-awareness
       with conceptual "knowing."

10.   People tend to believe in thought.

11.   Thinking is controlled by the ego
       and the ego uses thought to preserve its imaginary self.

12.   Therefore, to believe in thoughts, ideas and concepts,
including those thoughts that people imagine are their own,
is an error that results in failure to end the ego.

13.   Thoughts, ideas, beliefs, concepts, emotions and desires
are the fundamental tools the impostor self (ego) uses
to prevent you from directly experiencing your True Self.

14.   For those few individuals
       who are seriously intent on Liberation,
       it is essential to stop using thought
       as a means to know the absolute Truth.

15.   It is also essential to stop believing in thoughts, ideas,
and concepts; including those thoughts, ideas and concepts
you imagine being your own.

16.   Understanding the nature of beliefs can help one to see
that thought is not a means to know the absolute Truth.

17.   Seeing that thought is not a means
       to know the absolute Truth
       is the way to stop using thought
       as a means to know the absolute Truth.

18. There is a method you can try that reveals
    that thought is not a means to know the absolute Truth.

19. It is the "How Do You Know Method."

20. Here are the instructions for the
    How Do You Know Method (21-27):

21. Look at any belief you have.

22. Ask of that belief:
    "How do I know absolutely for sure this is true?"

23. The mind will give an answer.

24. To the answer the mind gives ask:
    "How do I know absolutely for sure this is true?"

25. Every time the mind gives an answer,
    question the answer by repeating the question:
    "How do I know absolutely for sure this is true?"

26. You must be willing to question
    every answer the mind gives for the method to work.

27. If you are willing to question every answer the mind
    gives to the question "How do I know absolutely
    for sure this is true?" the inquiry will always end in
    "I don't know absolutely for sure this is true".

28. The How Do You Know Method is an excellent way
    to see the difference between believing and knowing.

29.   The How Do You Know Method
        is also an excellent way to see
        that thought is not a means to know the absolute Truth.

30.   After questioning a few hundred beliefs using the
        How Do You Know Method, it should be quite clear
        that thought is not a means to know the absolute Truth.

31.   Thought is like a great pretense or house of cards.

32.   One idea is supported by another idea.

33.   The How Do You Know Method is a way to see that
        when you trace each idea back,
        you find there is actually no real foundation at all.

34.   There is another way to see that
thought is not a way to know the absolute Truth: understand
the nature of belief and concepts; see how belief is formed
and how the ego creates ideas that preserve its imaginary self.

35.   It is the "Arguing Both Sides Method".

36.   The Arguing Both Sides Method
        begins by looking at some belief you have,
        maybe one of the current issues of the day.

37.   Write an argument for your belief.

38.   Look at your belief and write up all the proofs,
        arguments, evidence, and reasons that support it.

39.   Next, pretend that you have the opposite belief
and write up all the proofs, arguments, evidence and reasons
that support that opposite belief.

40.   The purpose of the Arguing Both Sides Method
       is to demonstrate that thought can create
       reasons, evidence and support for any belief.

41.   Seeing that thought can create evidence and reasons
       to support any belief, is a very powerful key.

42.   The Arguing Both Sides Method
is another way of revealing that thought is really baseless.

43.   The Arguing Both Sides Method also demonstrates that
       thought forms conclusions based on motive.

44.   Evidence is not the primary factor that determines
       what conclusions and beliefs will be formed.

45.   Motivation is the primary factor
       in the forming of beliefs.

46.   Evidence will be gathered to support the motive.

47.   The ego will gather
       all the so-called evidence and reasons
       to support what the ego wants to believe.

48.   The ego's primary motive
       is to preserve its imaginary self.

49.   Therefore, the ego directs thought
to create concepts that will help to preserve its imaginary self.

50.   In almost all humans,
including almost all spiritual aspirants and students, the
desire of the ego to preserve its imaginary self is very strong.

51.   In almost all humans including almost all
        spiritual aspirants and students, the ego directs thought
        to create concepts that will preserve its imaginary self.

52.   One of the ego's preservation strategies
        is selecting spiritual teachings that are not direct.

53.   Even if one manages to find the Direct Path Teachings,
the ego will distort the Direct Path Teachings by interpreting
what is written or said in a way that supports the ego, or the
ego will distort the Direct Path Teachings by focusing on that
which is not essential.

54.   One of the tricks (ego preservation strategies) that the
ego uses most commonly with spiritual aspirants is to confuse
intellectual "spirituality" with authentic spirituality.

55.   Most people only have an intellectual interest
        in spiritual concepts and do not wish to end the ego.

56.   Most people just enjoy learning about the concepts.

57.   There are some people who realize
        their interest is only intellectual.

58.   There are other people who believe
       they have an interest in ending the ego,
       who do not really have an interest in ending the ego.

59.   Almost all of the people on a spiritual path that claims
       to have as its aim the ending of the ego illusion
       actually have very little desire to end the ego illusion.

60.   The way to end all of the ego's preservation strategies
       is to increase the desire for liberation.

61.   There are a few very condensed Direct Path Teachings
       that can be a great help on the Direct Path.

62.   You will find those Direct Path Teachings
       in the six books of this Self Realization series.

63.   However, to go on and on
reading thousands of spiritual or religious books and
discussing spiritual teachings is an ego preservation strategy
to keep you in the realm of thought instead of practice.

64.   All of the time you spend reading and discussing could
be better spent practicing the Awareness Watching Awareness
Method. That is assuming you have dropped all of your
unnecessary activities. If you have not dropped all of your
unnecessary activities to create the maximum amount of time
for the practice of the Awareness Watching Awareness
Method, then read all six of the books in the Self Realization
Series cover to cover, over and over again, until you do drop
all of your unnecessary activities to create the maximum
amount of time to practice Awareness Watching Awareness.

65.   Practice leads to Liberation.

66.   Endless reading of the
false spiritual or religious teachings from the past and
discussing spiritual or religious teachings leads to illusion.

67.   The ego creates arguments against the Direct Path
        as a preservation strategy.

68.   The ego calls indirect paths "direct paths"
        as an ego preservation strategy.

69.   Instead of spending all one's spare time in spiritual
practice, the ego finds almost endless ways to spend one's
spare time, and this is one of the ego's primary preservation
strategies. Some examples are television, entertainment,
reading, discussing, and thinking. The ego can find
thousands of ways to avoid spiritual practice.

70.   If you drop all of your unnecessary activities,
        you will have much more time for spiritual practice.

71.   One ego preservation strategy (one of the impostor's
tricks) is creating arguments against what is written here
instead of open-mindedly considering the possibility that
what is revealed in this book points towards the truth
that the ego prevents most people from seeing.

72.   Another ego preservation strategy (trick the impostor
uses) is deciding in advance that one of the methods described
in the Self Realization series of books will not work,
without ever giving the method a sincere try.

73. See how the ego directs every thought
    to create a way to preserve its imaginary self.

74. In other words, ask of every thought, idea, concept,
    belief, etc.: "Does this thought, idea, concept or belief
    help the ego illusion to continue?"

75. When you form a belief,
    you are no closer to discovering the absolute Truth
    than you were before you formed the belief.

76. When you form a belief, you have created an obstacle
    to discovering the absolute Truth.

77. If you were honest, instead of a belief,
    your view would be "I don't know."

78. If you really wanted Truth,
    you would insist on Direct Experience.

79. If you really wanted Truth, you would never accept
    a belief. A belief is only a group of symbols.
    All words are symbols.

80. The extremely intense desire for Liberation
is the key to ending the ego's tricks.
Book Two in the Self Realization Series *The Desire for Liberation*
contains step-by-step instructions for awakening
the extremely intense desire for Liberation.

81. Allow yourself to see how the impostor self
    has enslaved you by seeing its preservation strategies.

82.   Reading all six books in the Self Realization Series
        is a great first step towards conquering
        all of the obstacles the false self creates.

83.   Repeated reading, over and over, reflecting on each
sentence, is very important. If at some point in the future you
have dropped all unnecessary activities and are using all of
the free time thus created to practice the Awareness Watching
Awareness Method, then your time will be far better spent in
practice instead of reading. However, in the beginning, most
people need a foundation to motivate them to drop all
unnecessary activities to create the maximum amount of time
to practice, and thus in the beginning reading these authentic
Direct Path Teachings is very important.

84.   Your motivation while reading is very important.

85.   The correct motivations are (86-89):

86.   Extremely intense Self-honesty.

87.   An extremely intense desire to directly experience
        the infinite-eternal-absolute Truth.

88.   A willingness to let go of
        all the ideas you have accumulated in the past.

89.   An extremely intense longing to be free of sorrow
        and to live in eternal-joy.

90.   If the extremely intense desire for liberation is awakened in you it will bring everything you need to succeed at bringing the impostor self to its final end so that you can remain eternally as your true Self which is Absolutely Perfect Infinite-Awareness-Love-Bliss that has never experienced any sorrow or suffering in all of eternity.

91.   Remember the Two Great Keys to Self Realization:

A.   Awakening the extremely intense desire for Liberation.

B.   Self honesty. Self honesty begins by actually seeing the ego's preservation strategies.

92.   When the extremely intense desire for Freedom is awakened, clarity, sincerity, earnestness, insight and discernment are also awakened, and then you can see what is essential and what is not essential.

93.   The end of the ego is the end of all suffering and all sorrow for all eternity.

94.   The end of the ego is infinite-eternal-awareness-love-bliss.

95.   Realize that ending the ego is the only truly worthwhile event that can happen in a human life.

96.   Take a look at your actions moment by moment to see if they conform to the realization that ending the ego is the only truly valuable event that can happen in a human life.

97.   The ego projects thoughts and fantasies
      and the ego interprets.

98.   One way to stop this distortion is to ask "What is the false self doing right now to preserve its imaginary self?"

99.   Another way to stop the distortion is to ask, "Have I added a concept or interpretation to what I am reading?"

100. Most people project much thinking
      onto the teachings that they read.

101. Their thinking has very little to do
      with the teachings they have read.

102. Almost all humans are in a state of chaotic confusion.

103. Most people do not realize
      that they are in a state of chaotic confusion.

104. Interpreting what is written
      is an expression of that chaotic confusion.

105. Actually practicing 98 and 99 above
      can help greatly to end that distortion.

106. Almost everyone underestimates
      how deceptive the false self is.

107. The impostor self can be brought to its final end.

108. What remains is Absolutely-Perfect-Eternal-Love-Bliss.

Please use the contact form at seeseer.com to let us know if reading the book The False self was a good experience for you.

The six books in the Self Realization Series are:

1.   Self Awareness Practice Instructions.

The most direct and rapid means to Self Realization goes by various names including:

A.   Self Inquiry.
B.   Self Abidance.
C.   Self Attention.
D.   Self Awareness.
E.   Abiding as Awareness.
F.   Awareness of Awareness.
G.   Awareness Aware of Itself.
H.   Awareness Watching Awareness.

The book Self Awareness Practice Instructions contains all of the quotes in Chapter (Step) Seven from the book The Seven Steps to Awakening and also both Chapter Seven: Practice Instructions for the Awareness Watching Awareness Method and Chapter Eight: Further Clarification of the Awareness Watching Awareness Method from the book The Most Direct Means to Eternal Bliss.

2.   The Desire for Liberation.

The awakening of the extremely intense desire for Liberation is the most important aid to Self Realization. The book The Desire for Liberation contains all of the quotes in Chapter (Step) Four from the book The Seven Steps to Awakening and both Chapter Four: The Desire for Liberation and Chapter Five: How to Awaken the Extremely Intense Desire for Liberation from the book The Most Direct Means to Eternal Bliss.

3.   *The False self.*

The false self goes by many different names including:

A.   *Ego.*
B.   *Mind.*
C.   *Thinking*
D.   *A bundle of thoughts*
E.   *The impostor self.*

The book The False self contains all of the quotes in Chapter (Step) Three from the book The Seven Steps to Awakening. It also contains the contents of Chapter One: The Impostor, Chapter Two: The Impostor's Tricks and Chapter Three: The Impostor's Tools from the book The Most Direct Means to Eternal Bliss.

4.   *Inspiration and Encouragement*
       on the Path to Self Realization.

This collection of quotes is for the purpose of inspiring, encouraging and motivating those who are seeking Self Realization.

That includes being inspired, encouraged and motivated to:

A. Make and maintain the decision to bring the impostor self to its final end and thus to remain eternally as your true Self which is Absolutely Perfect Infinite-Awareness-Love-Bliss that has never experienced any sorrow or suffering in all of eternity.

B. Drop all of your unnecessary activities and use all of the free time thus created to practice the most direct and rapid means leading to Self Realization. The Seven Sages placed tremendous emphasis on the importance of practice.

The more times you read these quotes the better. Read all of these quotes every day, or at least be sure to read them every time you feel the need to be inspired, encouraged or motivated to get back on track in one-pointedness towards your spiritual goal and spiritual practice. The quotes in this book are the same as the quotes in Chapter (Step) Five from the book The Seven Steps to Awakening.

5.   Everything is an Illusion.

What is helpful about reading these types of quotes is that the more you can realize that everything is an illusion the better you can ignore everything and turn inward. One of the most significant aspects to this collection of quotes by the Sages is that in addition to pointing out that everything is a dreamlike illusion, they also point out in many of their quotes that upon Self Realization everything disappears. This book contains all of the quotes in Chapter (Step) Two from the book The Seven Steps to Awakening.

6.   How Not to Get Lost in Concepts.

A mistake made by almost everyone who studies the Direct Path teachings is that instead of using the teachings as practice instructions they become lost in spiritual concepts. Most of those people never correct that mistake and at the end of their physical life they are still lost in a maze of concepts without having realized the Self. This book contains all of the quotes in Chapter (Step) One from the book The Seven Steps to Awakening.

For more information about these books go to:

www.seeseer.com

CPSIA information can be obtained
at www.ICGtesting.com
Printed in the USA
LVOW08s0737030417

528892LV00010B/162/P